Published By Adam Gilbin

@ Tony Pinto

Dog Training: How to Housebreak Your Dog Easy

Guide to Raising a Happy and Well-behaved Dog

All Right RESERVED

ISBN 978-87-94477-71-0

TABLE OF CONTENTS

Chapter 1 1

Dog Training And Behavior 1

Chapter 2 14

The Basics Of The Language Of Dog 14

Chapter 3 28

Introduction To Dog Training 28

Chapter 4 31

Understanding Canine Nutrition 31

Nutritional Needs Of Dogs 31

Chapter 5 39

Applying General Preparation Standards. 39

Chapter 6 48

Getting Things Started 48

Chapter 7 78

Understanding Resource Guarding In French Bulldogs .. 78

Chapter 8 83

Preparing For Your New Puppy 83

Chapter 9 89

Accepting Health Care Prevention 89

Chapter 10 94

Dog Nutrition And Health 94

Nutritional Requirements 94

Chapter 11 107

Developing The Art Of Listening In Your Dog 107

Chapter 12 115

Getting To Know Your Dog 115

Chapter 13 118

Basic Techniques In Dog Treat Preparation 118

Baking Basics 118

NO-BAKE OPTIONS 121

Chapter 14 129

Instructing The "Tune In". 129

Chapter 15 133

Unwanted Behavior... 133

Chapter 1

Dog Training and Behavior

A crucial aspect of training your dog is teaching them basic commands. These commands provide a foundation for more complex training and enable you to communicate more effectively with your pet. Basic commands such as "sit," "stay," "come," and "heel" are essential for a well-behaved dog.

To teach your dog these commands, it is essential to use positive reinforcement and repetition. Offering treats and praise for correct responses can motivate your dog to want to learn and obey commands. Additionally, incorporating these commands into your everyday routine can help solidify their understanding and application.

When teaching your dog the "sit" command, begin by standing directly in front of your dog and holding a treat above their nose. Slowly move the treat upwards as your dog's head follows it. As their head lifts towards the treat, their bottom should lower to the ground. When your dog is in a seated position, offer them the treat and give praise.

To teach your dog the "stay" command, start by having them sit. Hold your open hand in front of their face and say "stay." Take a step back and immediately return to them, rewarding them with a treat and praise if they remain in place. Gradually increase the distance and duration of the "stay" command.

The "come" command is an essential safety command and can be taught by calling your dog's name followed by "come." Reward them with a treat and praise when they successfully respond to the command.

Finally, the "heel" command teaches your dog to walk alongside you without pulling on the leash. Begin by holding the leash in your left hand, with your dog on your left side. Use your right hand to hold a treat in front of them while saying "heel." Walk forward, and when your dog stays beside you, offer them the treat and praise.

By teaching your dog these basic commands, you can establish a strong foundation for more advanced training while ensuring that your dog is well-behaved in various situations.

House Training

House training your dog can sometimes be a challenging process, but it is necessary for living together in a healthy and harmonious environment. Consistency is key for successful house training. It is important to establish a routine for your dog?s meals and potty breaks.

During the house training process, it is also important to supervise your dog constantly. When you are unable to watch your dog, confine them to a small space or crate to prevent accidents from happening.

Positive reinforcement is the most effective method to house train your dog. Reward your dog with treats, praise, and affection after they have successfully gone potty outside. It is important to never punish your dog for accidents, as this can lead to fear and anxiety.

Accidents are bound to happen during the house training process. When they do, it is important to clean them up immediately and thoroughly. Using an enzymatic cleaner helps eliminate the odor, which can attract the dog to the same spot.

Remember, house training takes time and patience. It is important to have realistic expectations and continue to be consistent with your routine and positive reinforcement.

Barking and Whining

Barking and whining are natural forms of communication for dogs, but excessive barking and whining can be problematic for both the dog and their owner. Understanding the reasons behind the behavior is crucial in identifying the best training methods to address it.

Barking can be a sign of alerting their owner to potential danger, expressing anxiety or frustration, seeking attention, or simply out of boredom. Different types of barking should be treated differently. For example, alert barks can be reduced by teaching the dog a ?quiet? command or providing them with sufficient mental and physical stimulation to reduce their overactive impulses.

Whining, on the other hand, can indicate an emotional state such as anticipation, fear, or pain and discomfort. To reduce whining, owners should ensure that their basic needs such as food, water, and exercise are addressed, and assess for any underlying medical conditions.

Using positive reinforcement techniques such as treats, toys, and praise can be an effective way to teach dogs to reduce their barking and whining. It is important to note that punishment or physical force should never be used as it could exacerbate the problem and damage the dog?s trust in their owner.

In summary, as with any training, patience and consistent practice are the keys to success. With the proper knowledge and training techniques, excessive barking and whining can be minimized, resulting in a happy and healthy relationship between the dog and their owner.

Aggression

Aggression in dogs can be a serious issue and should be addressed as soon as it becomes apparent. It can be caused by a variety of factors including fear, territoriality, possessiveness, or even just learned behavior. Signs of aggression can include growling, biting, snarling, lunging, or even a stiff body posture.

It is important to address the root cause of the aggression, rather than just trying to suppress the behavior. Proper training and socialization can often help alleviate aggression. Positive reinforcement techniques such as clicker training can be effective in reinforcing desirable behavior and decreasing the likelihood of aggression.

In some cases, it may be necessary to consult with a professional dog trainer or behaviorist. They can help identify the root cause of the aggression and develop a customized training plan to address it. In extreme cases where the aggression poses a serious risk to others, it may be necessary to consult with a veterinarian about medication options or consider rehoming the dog to a more appropriate environment.

It is important to always prioritize safety when dealing with aggressive dogs. Make sure to take necessary precautions such as using a muzzle or keeping the dog away from unknown people or animals until the issue can be addressed.

Separation Anxiety

Separation anxiety is a common problem that many dogs experience. It occurs when dogs become anxious or panicked when they are separated from their owners. Signs of separation anxiety include excessive barking, destructive behavior, pacing, and inappropriate elimination.

Fortunately, there are steps that can be taken to help your dog overcome separation anxiety. One of the most effective ways is to gradually desensitize your dog to being left alone. By starting with short periods of time, such as a few minutes, and gradually increasing the time as your dog becomes more comfortable, you can teach your dog that being alone is not something to be feared.

Another way to help your dog with separation anxiety is to make sure that they get plenty of exercise and mental stimulation during the day. This can include going for walks, playing fetch, and giving them puzzle toys to play with.

In some cases, medication may be necessary to help with severe separation anxiety. It is important to work with a veterinarian or certified dog behaviorist to determine the best course of action for your dog.

With patience and consistency, it is possible to help your dog overcome separation anxiety and enjoy spending time alone.

Socialization

Socialization is a crucial part of a dog's development, as it helps ensure they're comfortable in a range of situations and around different people, dogs, and other animals. This process starts early, ideally when a puppy is between 3 and 16 weeks old. During this time, puppies are more open to new experiences and less likely to see them as threats.

Socialization should be a gradual process that introduces puppies to new people, sounds, textures, smells, and sights in a controlled manner. Puppy classes are a great way to introduce them to other puppies and learn basic commands. Additionally, exposing them to different people, including young children, adults, and seniors, will help ensure that they're well-socialized.

It's important to note that socialization is not just about making puppies comfortable around humans. It's also crucial to expose them to other animals, including different dog breeds, cats, and other pets, to help them learn how to act appropriately around them.

By properly socializing your dog, you can help ensure that they're well-adjusted, confident, and friendly, which will make your life and theirs much easier. Be patient and consistent, and don't be hesitant to seek guidance from a professional dog trainer if needed.

Chapter 2

The Basics of the Language of Dog

Perception and Interaction

As excited you may be about growing closer to your friend, there is one fact you should realize to avoid becoming disappointed while communicating with your dog or trying to wield the Language of Dog to train him: Your Dog isn't Human. Yes, he is more loving than many people you may have met in your life and he may have been with you through thick and thin, but you need to understand this fact before proceeding.

Canines think differently; unlike people who usually accept a leadership hierarchy, dogs tend to test the beings above them and realize that those below them will test their own dominance.

This is because they believe that only the strongest should be in charge or else their lives and those of the rest of the pack will be in danger. Besides, dogs love having rules to follow, something only strong leadership can set and command.

Since she's living with you, you'll be your dog's pack. However, in order for your relationship to succeed, you need to make sure that you're the pack's leader. To ascertain your dominance, you need to tend to your dog's needs and set limits in addition to showering her with love. If you think that's too harsh, remember that providing affections without rules goes against dogs' instincts, depriving them from becoming well-balanced, stable-minded, secure and happy.

Now you must be wondering where the logic in this is, but, again, dogs aren't human. They don't have the same reasoning skills you flaunt. Even their emotions are different since they lack complex thought. For instance, Rex may feel happy when you're happy while Tricia may show sadness when someone in your pack dies. However, they don't dwell on these emotions for long nor are they burdened with matters from the past. Thing is, if you do, they'll feel the unstable energy around you and consider you weak.

Another scenario where you may seem weak is if you're trying to comfort your dog during a tough time. By giving him a pat or even hugging him, you'll be telling your dog that it's okay to be in that current state of mind. However, this is considered a weakness because followers always look up to the Alpha Male to feed on their strength. So by showing affection rather than allowing him to solve his own situation, you'll be creating a problem that you won't be able to talk your way out of.

By showing your "weakness", your dog will instinctually take over and become the pack leader regardless of whether they want to or not. Dogs are quite responsible that way since they believe that the pack needs a strong leader, not one as sappy as you. However, by giving off these mixed signals, you'll be throwing him off balance, driving him to misbehave around the house or rebel through acts like chewing the furniture, leaving "gifts" inside your home, barking excessively, and refusing to abide by your commands. Even separation anxiety is the result of these mixed signals; if your dog believed that you were truly the pack leader, she wouldn't be all over the place. Pack leaders may come and go as they please whereas their followers should stick close. Aggression is also common in these situations since dogs may challenge your claims of dominance.

So, remember that your thoughts and emotions are different from those your pet experiences. You'll need to keep these in check to truly enjoy the communication you're gearing up to start.

Your Dog's Voice

As you know by now, dogs communicate mostly with their human companions through sound, a method they embraced after being domesticated. One admirable aspect is that dogs can use their vocal cords to emit different sound, but you'll need to know what each means in order to communicate effectively with them.

Barking

Barking is one of the main sounds your dog will make to alert you about something, sound an alarm of sorts, demand your attention (or food), signal its fear, suspicion and distress, or simply indicate that she's bored and wants to play. However, it's the tone of her barking which you should focus on.

When distressed, her bark will be high-pitched and repetitive. The more upset she grows, the higher her bark's pitch will be.

A bored dog' bark will be a repetitive monotone. Meanwhile, if she's demanding something, her barks will be more persistent, sharp and directed at you.

If scared or if she senses danger, her barks will be sharp and staccato-like. The bigger the threat, the more intense her barks will be.

If suspicious, she'll bark in a slow, low tone. However, if she's also scared, her barks will be low and faster.

If she's in a playful mood, well, you'll be able to determine her mood because everything about her will expose her intentions.

Baying

Baying, or a deep-throated barking that lasts longer than most, is one sound you may not hear often. This is because dogs usually bay whenever they're pursuing prey or if they're challenging an intruder. If you have a scent hound, rest assured that you'll experience a few melodic baying sounds sometimes.

Growling

Dogs growl to warn their owners or other dogs that an aggressive act is bound to happen if they don't back down or stop annoying them. Instead of being offended, make sure to take heed and later find a way to make him more comfortable. Keep in mind that dogs also growl whenever they're playing, especially as they tug on things. This is more acceptable, but you should make sure that the rest of your pet's body language indicates that he's just playing. On the other hand, if you have a Rottweiler, you can be at ease because this breed grumbles whenever happy.

Howling

If your dog is howling, chances are that it heard a high-pitched sound such as that of fire and police sirens. However, the main purpose of this sound is to connect pack members or locate them. Another meaning for howling is distress; your pet may feel isolated or distressed by separation.

Whimpering

If your dog whimpers or yelps, he's in pain. As a puppy, he used this vocal cue whenever his brothers and sisters bit him too hard. It's also another way of showing that he's distressed or too excited. If it's the latter, expect licking, jumping and barking as well.

Whining

This is another high-pitched sound which dogs make through their noses. She'll whine if she needs something from you or if she has been separated from someone. Basically, it's a way for her to voice her stress.

Facial Expressions

Dogs use their ears, mouths and eyes to express their emotions just like humans do. However, these expressions go and come quickly, which is why you need to be very attentive to catch them. Here's a quick look at the

Aggression

If a dog is aggressive, his eyes will either be narrowed down or staring challengingly. As for his ears, they will either be flattened against his head or pointed forward or back. Meanwhile, his lips will be drawn to show off his teeth, which may be snapping depending on how angry he is.

Scared

Whenever a dog is scared, her eyes will be narrowed and she'll try to avert the other dog or person's gaze. If too scared, she may even have her eyes rolled back in her head. Meanwhile, her ears will flat against her head while her lips will be drawn to show her teeth.

Too Scared and Ready to Escape

As she's getting ready to run away, her eyes will be open wide or rolled back into her head. Her ears will be back while drool spills from her slightly opened mouth.

Friendly

If she's in a good, friendly mood, her eye will be open wide, her ears perked up, and her mouth relaxed. You may even see a "smile".

Defensive

If she senses danger and goes in a guarding mode, her eyes will be open and alert, her ears up and forward, and her teeth bared. She may even snap with her teeth if very scared.

Playful

Also known to denote happiness, your dog's eyes will be wide and sparkly, his ears relaxed or perked up, and his mouth slightly open with no sign of his teeth.

Submissive

In front of an alpha, your do will show the signs of being submissive: narrowed eyes or wide open with whites showing, flattened ears, and mouth forming a grin while nuzzling the dominator.

Chapter 3

Introduction to Dog Training

The Importance of Training

Why is training crucial for your dog's well-being? In this section, we'll explore the benefits of training, ranging from creating a harmonious household to ensuring the safety of your dog and those around them. Understanding the significance of training lays the foundation for a positive and successful training journey.

Setting Expectations

Before diving into **the** training process, it's essential to set realistic expectations. This section guides you through understanding your dog's capabilities, the time commitment involved, and the gradual nature of the learning process. We'll discuss the patience required and the rewarding outcomes that come with consistent effort.

Establishing a Positive Training Mindset

Training is not just about teaching commands; it's about building a positive relationship with your dog. This part of the chapter focuses on cultivating a positive training mindset. Learn how your attitude, patience, and enthusiasm play pivotal roles in creating a training environment where your dog feels motivated and eager to learn.

Building a Connection with Your Dog

Training is a shared journey. This section emphasises the importance of building a strong connection with your dog. We'll explore activities and exercises that enhance the bond between you and your furry friend, laying the groundwork for effective communication and cooperation throughout the training process.

As you embark on this introductory chapter, envision the exciting possibilities that await you and your dog on this training adventure. Get ready to unlock the potential within your canine companion and foster a relationship built on trust, understanding, and mutual respect!

Chapter 4

Understanding Canine Nutrition

Nutritional Needs of Dogs

Understanding the nutritional needs of dogs is essential to giving them with a healthy and varied diet, including treats. Dogs, like people, require a mix of important nutrients to thrive. Here's a breakdown of the key nutritional factors important for your canine companion:

Protein: Protein is important for muscle growth, immune function, and general energy. High-quality animal-based foods, such as chicken, beef, and fish, are excellent picks. For dogs with specific dietary restrictions, plant-based proteins like beans and chickpeas can be considered.

Fats: Fats are important for keeping good skin and coat, as well as supporting different bodily processes. Include sources of healthy fats in your dog's food, such as fish oil, flaxseed, and lean meats. However, moderation is key to avoid weight-related problems.

Carbohydrates: Carbohydrates provide a source of energy. Opt for whole grains like brown rice and quinoa, as well as veggies such as sweet potatoes and carrots. Avoid large amounts of simple sugars, which can add to weight gain.

Vitamins: Dogs need a range of vitamins for different physiological processes. Ensure your dog gets adequate vitamins from fruits and veggies.

Vitamin-rich alternatives include blueberries, spinach, and apples.

Minerals: Essential minerals like calcium, phosphorus, and potassium play a key role in bone health, blood clotting, and brain function. Dairy goods, leafy greens, and meats are great sources.

Water: Adequate hydration is often ignored but is important for digestion, temperature control, and general well-being. Always provide fresh, clean water for your dog.

Special Considerations: Consider your dog's age, size, and exercise level when considering nutritional needs. Puppies, adults, and active breeds may require changes in their food to support their unique life stage.

Key Ingredients for Healthy Treats

When it comes to making healthy treats, the choice of ingredients is important. The goal is to make treats that not only taste great but also add to your dog's overall health. Here are key items to include in your handmade dog treats:

Lean Proteins: Incorporate lean proteins like chicken, turkey, and fish into your treat recipes. These proteins help muscle development and provide important amino acids.

Whole Grains: Opt for whole grains such as oats, brown rice, and quinoa. These foods offer a good source of energy and fiber, promoting gut health.

Fruits and Vegetables: Include dog-friendly fruits and vegetables rich in vitamins and minerals. Blueberries, carrots, and sweet potatoes are not only healthy but also add natural sweetness to treats.

Peanut Butter: Peanut butter is a favorite among dogs and can be a good source of fats and energy. Choose natural, unsalted peanut butter without extra sugars or fake sweeteners.

Greek Yogurt: Greek yogurt is rich in probiotics, supporting gut health. It's a tasty addition to frozen treats and offers a creamy feel.

Coconut Oil: Coconut oil offers a source of healthy fats and can add to a shiny coat. Introduce it in moderation due to its calorie density.

Eggs: Eggs are a flexible food rich in protein. They also provide vital protein acids and vitamins.

Flaxseed: Flaxseed is a good source of omega-3 fatty acids, promoting a healthy coat and face. Grind flaxseed to improve digestibility.

Chickpea Flour: For dogs with grain sensitivities, chickpea flour can be an acceptable option. It's gluten-free and adds a nutty taste to treats.

Applesauce: Unsweetened applesauce adds wetness to treats and offers a natural sweetness without extra sugars.

Common Allergens and Substitutes

Recognizing common allergens is crucial when making treats for your dog, especially if they have known allergies. Here are some common allergies and possible substitutes:

Wheat and Gluten: For dogs with wheat or gluten issues, try using alternative flours like rice flour, oat flour, or chickpea flour in your recipes.

Dairy: If your dog is lactose intolerant, opt for lactose-free options like coconut milk or almond milk instead of traditional dairy products.

Peanuts: Dogs can be allergic to peanuts. In such cases, switch peanut butter with almond butter or sunflower seed butter.

Eggs: For dogs with egg allergies, applesauce or mashed bananas can serve as binding agents in recipes.

Meat Proteins: In cases of meat allergies, consider lean, new proteins like venison or duck as replacements.

Fish: If your dog is allergic to fish, seek different forms of omega-3 fatty acids such as flaxseed or chia seeds.

By knowing the nutritional needs of dogs and selecting the right ingredients for your treats, you're not only ensuring a tasty reward for your furry friend but also contributing to their general health and well-being. Be mindful of possible allergens and make suitable substitutions to meet your dog's individual dietary needs. The next parts of this cookbook will delve into actual applications of these concepts, offering a range of recipes to fit different tastes and nutritional needs.

Chapter 5

Applying General Preparation Standards.

Manage your assumptions and state of mind.

Don't get angry or take it out on your dog because not every training day will be perfect. Change your own way of behaving and mentality to energize your canine's capacity and certainty to learn. In most cases, your dog will follow suit if you are at ease.

On the off chance that the canine becomes terrified of your awful state of mind, s/he won't learn anything new. He or she will only come to distrust you and be cautious.

You can improve your behavior and have success with your dog by taking dog training classes and working with a skilled trainer.

Remember your canine's personality.

Every dog has a unique temperament. Different breeds learn in different ways and at different rates, just like children. A few canines are obstinate and will challenge you every step of the way. People will do anything to please you. Your dog's temperament may necessitate that you modify your methods of training.

Give quick rewards.

Canines don't see long haul cause and impacts. They catch on quickly. To reinforce a desired behavior, you must praise or reward your dog within two seconds. He or she will not associate the reward with the action you asked him to perform if you wait too long.

In addition, you must ensure that your praise is delivered accurately and quickly. If you don't, you might reward undesirable behaviors.

Envision, for instance, that you are showing your canine the "sit" order. He or she sits for a brief moment, but by the time you praise and reprimand them, they have begun to stand up again. You are rewarding the standing behavior in this instance, not the sitting behavior. Be predictable. If there isn't consistency in your dog's environment, he or she won't understand what you want from them. Your dog's training objectives should be understood by everyone who lives with him or her. If you're training your dog not to jump on people, for instance, don't let the kids let the dog jump on them all the time. All of your training will be ruined by this.

Ensure everybody utilizes the specific orders your canine learns in preparing. S/he cannot tell the difference between "sit" and "sit down" because they do not speak English. He or she will only be confused if you use those terms interchangeably.

Since s/he won't make an unmistakable association between a solitary order and a solitary activity, his/her reaction to the order will be all in or all out.

Take a look at clicker training.

Clicker preparing is a strategy for conveying prompt recognition with the assistance of a clicker. You can click quicker than you can give a treat or pet your canine's head. Thusly, clicker preparing builds up appropriate conduct quickly enough for a canine's learning speed. It works by making a positive relationship between the snap sound and rewards. Your dog will eventually consider the clicker's sound as a sufficient reward for good behavior. You can apply the guideline of clicker preparing to any canine order.

Give the dog a treat right away after you click the clicker. This makes a positive relationship with the snap sound. That sound will later "mark" a correct behavior, letting the dog know that he or she did something right.

Give the dog a treat and a click when he does something you want him to do. You can give the behavior a command name once s/he consistently exhibits it. Utilizing the clicker, get started tying the behavior and command together.

For instance, before you ever teach your dog the "sit" command, give him or her a treat, make a click sound, and praise them when they sit. At the point when s/he starts sitting just to get the treats, begin giving the signal "sit" to get him/her into position. To reward them, pair it with the click sound. At some point, he or she will come to understand that sitting in response to the "sit" command will result in a click reward.

Always give praise and occasionally a small treat for success and good behavior.

Little treats assist with propelling your canine to become familiar with his/her preparation. The snack must be small, tasty, and simple to chew.

You don't want it to stop the training or make them overly full.

Think about how much longer it takes to chew a dry treat like "Bill Jack" or "Zuke's Mini Naturals" compared to a hard one. You won't have to wait long for your dog to eat the treats, which are about the size of a pencil eraser's head.

Use "high worth" treats when required.

Use a "high value" treat to make the command more difficult or important for the student. Models incorporate freeze-dried liver, cooked chicken bosom pieces, or cuts of turkey lunch meat.

As the canine learns the order, gradually eliminate the high worth treats and bring them back depending on the situation to propel your preparation, yet consistently give him/her commendation.

Train while starving.

Try not to take care of as huge a feast as expected a couple of hours prior to preparing your canine. The more your dog wants the treat, the more focused he or she will be on the task at hand.

Continuously finish strong.

Regardless of whether the instructional meeting work out positively and your canine didn't get on to another order, end on something that you can laud him/her for. The last thing he or she will remember is your love and praise if you end the training session with a command he or she already knows.

Discourage barking.

If your dog barks at you when you don't want him or her to, ignore him or her until he or she stops, after which you should praise him or her. They may bark at you for attention at times, or they may do so out of frustration.

Don't throw a toy or ball. This merely teaches him or her that if they bark, they will get you to do what they want.

The dog will be rewarded with attention if you yell at him or her to be quiet.

Chapter 6

Getting Things Started

To begin the process of teaching a German Shepherd, a firm foundation must be established through a systematic and patient approach. The first stage is to create a learning environment that is conducive to learning.

Choose a calm, distraction-free location where both you and the dog can concentrate. This establishes the foundation for efficient communication throughout training sessions.

Next, become acquainted with positive reinforcement approaches. German Shepherds respond favorably to incentives, praise, and toys. Use these rewards to promote desired actions. To develop a clear association, be consistent with the incentives, ensuring they are delivered soon following the proper activity.

Understanding the breed-specific characteristics of German Shepherds is critical.

Recognize their wisdom, dedication, and drive to please. Customize your training approaches to favorably leverage these features.
 To avoid boredom, engage them in cognitively engaging activities. Boredom can lead to undesired actions.

Basic instructions like sit, remain, and come should be taught gradually. Begin with short sessions to keep the dog interested and progressively increase the time as they improve.

Always use a firm yet gentle tone, and be patient. Consistency is essential in reinforcing orders and developing a routine that the German Shepherd can understand.

Socialization is an important part of training. To enhance adaptation and lessen potential aggressiveness, expose your German Shepherd to a variety of situations, people, and other animals.

Controlled encounters will assist children in developing excellent manners and reducing nervousness in various settings.

Include leash training from the start to develop good walking behavior. This not only secures your dog's obedience but also encourages a healthy exercise regimen.

Regular walks give both physical and cerebral stimulation, resulting in a well-balanced and pleased German Shepherd.

Finally, be aware of your German Shepherd's unique demands and characteristics. Adapt the training method to their temperament and energy levels.

Regular progress evaluation allows for changes in the training routine, assuring a happy and gratifying learning experience for both you and your canine partner.

Choosing a Puppy German Shepherd

To create a happy match between the dog and its future owner, selecting a German Shepherd puppy demands careful thought. Begin by looking into the breeder's reputation and the puppy's pedigree.

Reputable breeders promote health and temperament, checking for hereditary disorders as needed. Request to meet the puppy's parents in order to assess their behavior and provide a safe environment.

Examine the litter dynamics to get a puppy that fits your lifestyle. German Shepherds are well-known for their intelligence and adaptability, making them ideal for a variety of tasks ranging from family companions to working dogs.

Look for evidence of confidence, curiosity, and friendliness in the puppy's disposition. Stay away from extremes of shyness or violence.

Physical qualities are important; look for indicators of health in the puppy's coat, ears, and eyes. A puppy with clean eyes and a well-kept coat is a sign of sound breeding techniques.

Ascertain that the breeder offers the necessary immunizations and paperwork.

Consider your living circumstances and degree of exercise. German Shepherds flourish when they are regularly exercised and mentally stimulated.

Examine the puppy's accessible area as well as your commitment to daily walks and play. A German Shepherd that has been exercised is more likely to demonstrate positive behavior.

Selecting a German Shepherd puppy requires balancing health, temperament, and lifestyle concerns. Spend time researching, visiting reputable breeders, and selecting a puppy that matches your goals and talents to ensure a happy and long-lasting friendship.

Taking the Dog Home

Bringing a German Shepherd into your house is the start of an exciting adventure with one of the most intelligent and loyal dog breeds.

Begin by establishing a distinct area with comfortable beds and the necessary materials.

Establish a regular feeding regimen that includes a balanced meal that meets the nutritional requirements of the breed.

Training is essential for a well-mannered German Shepherd. Begin with simple commands such as sit, remain, and come.

Positive reinforcement, such as food and praise, can help you and your new companion form a deep relationship. German Shepherds thrive on cerebral stimulation, so keep them entertained with interactive play and puzzle toys.

A well-adjusted German Shepherd requires socialization. From a young age, expose them to a variety of surroundings, people, and other animals. This boosts confidence and lowers the probability of behavioral difficulties.

This lively breed requires plenty of exercise. Include regular walks, runs, and playtime to keep them both physically and intellectually occupied.

Obedience training should include leash etiquette to ensure a safe and comfortable walking experience.

The cornerstone of German Shepherd training is consistency. Positive actions should be constantly reinforced, while negative behaviors should be addressed as soon as possible. If necessary, seek expert training to lay the groundwork for a peaceful connection between you and your German Shepherd. You will have a well-behaved and loving companion for years to come if you invest time and effort in their training.

Knowing How to Communicate With your Dog

When it comes to teaching a German Shepherd, effective communication is essential. It is critical to understand your dog's body language, vocalizations, and individual personality.

Begin by forming a strong relationship with pleasant interactions such as playing and rewards. Consistency is essential in communicating expectations; employ clear, succinct orders; and promptly reinforce desired behaviors.

German Shepherds thrive on structure and regularity, so establish a regular training regimen.

Positive reinforcement can be used to reward excellent conduct with sweets or praise.

Gradually reinforce orders, making sure your dog knows each stage before moving on. Patience is essential; instead of punishing undesirable conduct, divert it to more acceptable acts.

Learn to interpret your dog's indications to determine their degree of comfort and tension.

Tail wagging, ear position, and general posture can all give useful information. Adjust your training strategy to ensure a good and stress-free learning environment.

Incorporate a variety of training techniques, such as obedience orders, agility exercises, and socializing.

Participate in engaging activities that engage both the intellect and the body, resulting in a well-rounded and content German Shepherd. Consider taking professional training programs or seeking guidance from expert trainers to better understand canine behavior.

Effective communication with your German Shepherd requires developing trust, consistency, and a thorough grasp of your dog's unique requirements.

You may develop a peaceful and well-trained companion by creating a deep connection and using positive reinforcement tactics.

Socialization of Your Puppy

Socialization is essential for your German Shepherd puppy's general growth and disposition.

Begin early by introducing your puppy to a variety of situations, people, and animals. This assists them in developing into well-adjusted adults.

Begin with gradual exposure to friendly pets and humans to ensure favorable encounters. Gradually introduce them to new noises, sights, and textures. This reduces anxiety and dread in unexpected circumstances.

Enroll your pet in puppy lessons for organized socializing. These sessions provide regulated environments for pups and humans to interact. In a group situation, your German Shepherd learns important instructions and good conduct.
 Introduce your puppy to a variety of situations, such as parks, streets, and crowded locations. This promotes adaptation and minimizes anxiety in a variety of scenarios.

Supervise interactions with youngsters to guarantee pleasant experiences and the prevention of fear-related behavior problems.

Playdates with other well-behaved dogs improve social skills. Monitor their body language and intervene if necessary to guarantee healthy encounters. Positive reinforcement during socializing, such as rewards and praise, encourages positive conduct.

Training a German Shepherd requires consistency. Make socializing a good and continuing experience by incorporating it into everyday activities. A well-socialized German Shepherd develops into a confident, well-behaved companion who thrives in a variety of contexts.

Why should you socialize your puppy?

Socializing your puppy is essential while training a German Shepherd for a variety of reasons. For starters, it encourages appropriate conduct and minimizes the possibility of violence.

Exposing your puppy to new people, surroundings, and animals helps them develop confidence and flexibility, which are important qualities in a well-behaved German Shepherd.

Second, socializing improves communication abilities. Your puppy learns to analyze body language, recognize cues, and behave correctly by engaging with a variety of stimuli.

This is especially vital for a breed like the German Shepherd, which is noted for its intellect and loyalty.

Furthermore, socializing helps with emotional

well-being. Positive early growth experiences lay the groundwork for a secure and happy adult dog.

Because German Shepherds are extremely devoted and protective, they benefit enormously from learning to distinguish between friend and foe via exposure to a variety of social situations.

Furthermore, socializing your puppy helps to reduce fear-based behavior disorders. A well-socialized German Shepherd is less prone to develop anxiety or hostility when confronted with new situations.

This is critical in order to provide a safe and pleasurable environment for both the dog and its owner.

Socializing your puppy is an important part of German Shepherd training. It builds a strong behavioral foundation, improves communication skills, promotes emotional well-being, and prevents fear-based problems. By putting time and effort into early socialization, you are not only sculpting a well-mannered companion, but also fostering a happy bond between you and your German Shepherd.

How to Make Friends

Developing deep bonds with a German Shepherd requires patience, consistency, and an awareness of their distinct features. Start by building trust through pleasant interactions.

Spend quality time together, participating in activities such as play and exercise, to strengthen your relationship.

Training must be done on a regular basis. German Shepherds are bright and thrive in a structured environment. Teach fundamental commands like sit, stay, and come, and reward them with positive reinforcement like food or praise.

To build a well-rounded temperament, socialize your dog from a young age by introducing them to a variety of situations, people, and other animals.

It is critical to understand the breed's protective instincts. While they become faithful friends, early training aids in the management of any guarding tendencies.

To avoid any anxiety, introduce new individuals gradually and positively.

Regular exercise is crucial for the physical and emotional well-being of a German Shepherd.

In order to boost their mind, provide activities like frequent walks, games, and puzzle toys. A dog who gets enough exercise is more likely to be well-behaved and social.

Make it possible for your German Shepherd to socialize with other dogs and humans in safe surroundings. Dog parks, training programs, and playdates can help to develop social skills and confidence. Friendship with a German Shepherd requires continuous training, socialization, and awareness of their distinct characteristics. Patience and positive reinforcement are critical to developing a deep relationship with these bright and devoted friends.

Educating your puppy on Basic Socializing Techniques

To train a German Shepherd puppy in basic socializing techniques, start with early and positive exposure to various environments, people, and other animals.

Begin by introducing your puppy to different sights, sounds, and textures to build their confidence. Socialization is crucial during the first few months of a German Shepherd's life to prevent fearfulness or aggression.

Expose your puppy to various people, including children, adults, and strangers, to ensure they become well-adjusted and friendly.

Teach them to interact gently and positively with different individuals. Likewise, expose them to different animals to promote positive associations and prevent aggressive behavior towards other pets.

Enroll your German Shepherd in puppy socialization classes where they can learn to interact with other dogs in a controlled environment.

These classes also provide an opportunity for you to refine their obedience skills. Consistency is key in training; establish a routine for walks, playtime, and training sessions to reinforce positive behavior.

Teach basic commands such as sit, stay, and come, using positive reinforcement like treats or praise.

German Shepherds are intelligent and eager to please, making them responsive to training. Additionally, use leash training to instill proper behavior during walks and public outings.

By prioritizing early and positive exposure to diverse experiences, people, and animals, you'll foster a well-socialized German Shepherd that is confident, friendly, and well-behaved in various situations.

Dos and Don'ts of Socializing

Socialization is essential for a German Shepherd's overall growth and disposition. Here are some important dos and don'ts for good socialization:

Dos:

Begin socializing with your German Shepherd Puppy as soon as possible. Begin socializing your German Shepherd puppy as soon as possible.

To develop good connections, expose them to a variety of situations, humans, and other animals.

Positive Reinforcement: Reward positive conduct with treats and praise during social encounters. Positive reinforcement enables your dog to link socialization with pleasant experiences.
Introduce your German Shepherd to a variety of

locations, such as parks, urban settings, and peaceful regions. This enables them to adjust to new environments and remain calm in a variety of scenarios.

Gradual Exposure: Introduce new people and animals to your dog gradually. Begin in safe conditions and work your way up to more difficult ones. This keeps your German Shepherd from being overwhelmed.

Socialization and obedience training should be combined. Teaching your dog basic instructions guarantees that he can navigate social situations with ease and listen to your directions.

Don'ts:

Avoid using force or overpowering your dog in encounters. Allow children to approach new circumstances at their own speed in order to provide a favorable experience. Negative Reinforcement: Avoid disciplining your German Shepherd when he is socializing. Negative experiences might cause fear or aggressiveness, impeding socialization.

Uncontrolled Meetings: Avoid uncontrolled encounters with unknown canines. Choose planned introductions to avoid disagreements and promote great connections.

Skipping socializing: Never underestimate the value of ongoing socializing. Exposure to new situations on a regular basis should be part of your dog's continuing training schedule.

You'll establish the groundwork for a well-socialized and confident German Shepherd by adhering to these dos and don'ts, fostering a strong link between you and your canine friend.

Promoting Good Behavior and Discouraging Negative behavior

A balanced and positive approach is essential while teaching a German Shepherd to encourage good conduct and discourage bad behavior. Begin by setting regular orders and rewards to develop clear communication.

When the dog performs desirable actions such as sitting or remaining, use positive reinforcement such as cookies or praise. This establishes a positive relationship, encouraging the dog to repeat similar behaviors.

Focus on redirection rather than punishment to discourage undesirable conduct. If your dog exhibits undesirable behavior, transfer their focus to a more appropriate activity. For example, if they begin chewing on furniture, provide them with a chew toy as an alternative.

In training, consistency is essential. Consistently enforce directives and ensure that all family members understand the norms and expectations.

German Shepherds thrive on regularity and structure, so sticking to a training program helps them grasp limits.

Socialization is essential for preventing bad behaviors such as aggressiveness and excessive barking.

From an early age, expose the dog to a variety of surroundings, humans, and other animals. This assists kids in being well-adjusted and less prone to engaging in scary or violent conduct.

Finally, patience is required. German Shepherds are bright and eager to please, but it takes time to teach them. Punishment-based techniques should be avoided since they might cause fear and anxiety.

Instead, concentrate on establishing a solid link via pleasant interactions, laying the groundwork for a well-behaved and happy German Shepherd.

Encourage Excellent Behavior while Discouraging Negative Behavior.

A balanced approach is essential for efficiently training a German Shepherd, stressing positive rewards for great conduct while discouraging undesirable behavior.

Positive reinforcement is the practice of rewarding desired behaviors with sweets, praise, or toys. When your German Shepherd shows excellent behavior, such as obeying or following directions, quickly praise them to reinforce the positive relationship.

Consistency is essential in deterring bad conduct. Respond to undesired acts quickly and assertively, shifting their attention to acceptable options. For example, if your German Shepherd chews on an inappropriate object, replace it with a chew toy and provide positive reinforcement when they use it.

Establish clear communication by issuing directives and providing consistent indications.

Create a deep link between you and your dog by reinforcing positive actions with vocal praise and physical love. Encourage positive conduct by using a strong and calm tone and diverting their attention to positive acts.

It is critical to implement an organized training program. Short training sessions on a regular basis assist in retaining attention and minimizing boredom.

Introduce variation to keep your German Shepherd's training interesting and intriguing, boosting excitement for learning. Remember that patience is essential. Positive reinforcement works effectively with dogs, and they will eventually link good behavior with incentives.

You can raise a well-behaved and happy German Shepherd by setting a positive training environment and frequently addressing undesirable habits.

Chapter 7

Understanding Resource Guarding in French Bulldogs

Understanding Resource Guarding in French Bulldogs: A Deeper Dive.

Resource guarding is a behaviour observed in many dogs, including French Bulldogs, that involves defending or protecting valued items from perceived threats. These items can range from food and toys to favourite resting spots or even human attention.

While resource guarding is a **natural** canine behaviour rooted in survival instincts, by understanding its dynamics and addressing it appropriately is crucial for fostering a harmonious relationship between pets and their owners.

Resource guarding is a common behaviour in French Bulldogs, rooted in their evolutionary history and individual characteristics. While it may pose challenges, understanding the nature of resource guarding allows owners to address it effectively.

The Nature of Resource Guarding

At its core, resource guarding is an instinctual response shaped by a dog's evolutionary history. In the wild, the ability to guard resources such as food, shelter, and mates was crucial for survival. Domestic dogs, despite their transformation from wild ancestors, retain this behaviour to varying degrees. In the context of a household, resource guarding may manifest as a dog becoming possessive or defensive when it perceives a threat to something it values.

Triggers for Resource Guarding

Several factors can trigger resource guarding behaviour in French Bulldogs:

Scarcity Mentality: Dogs, particularly those with a history of scarcity or competition for resources, may be more prone to guarding what they have.

Lack of Socialization: Insufficient exposure to various stimuli during the critical socialization period can contribute to fear or anxiety, leading to resource guarding as a defensive response.

Genetic Predisposition: Certain breeds, including French Bulldogs, may have a genetic predisposition to exhibit resource guarding behaviours. Understanding the breed's traits and tendencies is crucial in addressing these behaviours effectively.

Why French Bulldogs Exhibit Resource Guarding?

Territorial Nature

French Bulldogs, like many other dog breeds, have a territorial instinct that can contribute to resource guarding. They may view their living space, toys, or even their owners as part of their territory that needs protection. Understanding and respecting their need for personal space is key to managing resource guarding tendencies.

Affectionate Attachment

French Bulldogs are known for their affectionate and loyal nature. While this endearing quality fosters strong bonds with their owners, it can also lead to a desire to guard their humans or possessions as a way of expressing devotion. Balancing affection with clear boundaries is crucial in addressing this behaviour.

Chapter 8

Preparing for Your New Puppy

Choosing the Right Breed for Your Lifestyle

Research, Research, Research: Start by researching different dog breeds. Consider the size, energy level, and temperament that would be the best fit for your lifestyle. Remember, each breed has its unique traits.

Consider Adoption: Don't forget to check your local shelters and rescue organizations. There are many wonderful dogs in need of homes.

Consult with Breeders or Shelters: If you're considering a specific breed or a mixed-breed puppy, consult with breeders or shelters to gather more information about the puppies available.

Puppy-Proofing Your Home

Get Down to Puppy Level: To identify potential hazards, get down on your hands and knees and see your home from a puppy's perspective. Look for electrical cords, small objects, and toxic plants.

Essential Supplies and Equipment

Food and Water Bowls

Purchase durable, non-tip bowls made of stainless steel or ceramic.

Quality Puppy Food:

Consult with your vet to choose the right food for your puppy's age and breed. Start with the food the breeder or shelter was using and transition gradually if needed.

Collar and Leash

Choose a lightweight collar and leash. Make sure the collar has an ID tag with your contact information.

Crate or Puppy Pen:

A crate or puppy pen is an essential tool for housebreaking and providing a safe space for your puppy.

.Toys:

Get a variety of toys to keep your puppy engaged and help with teething.

Puppy Bed or Blankets:

Provide a comfortable place for your puppy to rest.

Grooming Supplies:

Depending on the breed, you might need brushes, shampoos, and nail clippers.

Cleaning Supplies:

Be prepared for accidents with pet-safe cleaning products.

Training Treats:

Invest in high-quality training treats to motivate your puppy during training sessions.

Puppy Proof the Yard:

If you have a yard, ensure it's secure and free of any potential escape routes.

Remember, your puppy will explore the world with their mouth, so remove anything small enough to swallow or chew on from their reach. As you set up your puppy's living space, think about what you'd need as a curious, energetic, and growing pup.

By carefully preparing your home and selecting the right supplies, you're laying the groundwork for a positive and safe environment that will help your puppy flourish. Now that your home is ready, the next step is to welcome your new family member and begin the journey of raising a well-behaved dog.

Chapter 9

Accepting Health Care Prevention

Establishing the Scene: Recognizing the Strong Bond

The relationship between people and dogs goes beyond the commonplace, whether it is in the quiet moments of a shared look or the joyful exuberance of a tail-wagging greeting. It is a friendship that has withstood the test of time, knitted into the fabric of our common past. Before we dive into the world of preventive healthcare, let's first recognize how strong this connection is. Our devoted companions, dogs, have played a significant role in human history as healers, protectors, and companions. The obligation to take care of our four-legged pets originates from this tapestry of shared moments.

Every gentle pat on the back or scratch behind the ears has an unwritten treaty that unites people from different countries and backgrounds. The language of dog friendship transcends all boundaries, be it the busy streets of Tokyo, the tranquil scenery of the Scottish Highlands, or the energetic markets of Marrakech. It's a language shared by all that mumbles stories of fidelity, tenacity, and the enduring link between people and their dogs.

The Heart of Prevention: A Harmony of Health and Welfare

One motif that stands out in this fabric of friendship is the desire of wellbeing. It involves more than just seeing to our dogs' medical needs when they become unwell; it involves creating a preventive care story in which every action is a note in a symphony of wellbeing. The core of preventive health care is like a soft tune that keeps on playing over time, making sure that our pets have long lives but also lives full of energy and happiness.

Our dedication to giving our dog friends the best possible life is embodied in preventive health care. It is a vow to be proactive, to anticipate their needs before disease comes on the door. Preventive health care guides a dog's life to produce a symphony of health, energy, and happiness, much like a maestro guides each instrument in an orchestra to make a harmonic piece.

International Link: Dog Friendship Is Unbound

The universality of the language of well-being becomes apparent as we explore the domains of preventative health care. The paw prints left on Mumbai's busy marketplaces are echoed in the streets of New York. The communal delight of playing fetch in a suburban garden reverberates throughout the rural landscapes of the Amazon rainforest and the skyscrapers of Hong Kong.

Fundamentally, canine companionship is a universal language that is spoken by billions of people. Dogs are loved members of every human family, no matter where they live—in the heart of Africa or the frigid depths of Antarctica. This manual serves as a bridge that links dog owners all across the world—it's more than just words on a page. It recognizes that the love and responsibility we have for our pets is what unites us, despite our differences in culture and location.

By acknowledging this worldwide link, we reveal the tapestry of canine companionship—a shared canvas adorned with the colors of love, care, and a dedication to safeguarding the welfare of our beloved pets—that transcends national boundaries. May this guide serve as a beacon for us as we navigate the upcoming chapters, showing the way toward a day when preventive health care is sung by caregivers everywhere as a global song.

Chapter 10

Dog Nutrition and Health

Nutritional Requirements

Dogs have specific nutritional requirements that must be met in order for them to maintain good health. These requirements vary depending on the dog's size, breed, activity level, and age. Regardless of these factors, all dogs need a balanced diet that includes protein, carbohydrates, fats, vitamins, and minerals.

Protein is essential for building and repairing tissues in the body. Dogs require higher levels of protein than humans do, and their sources of protein should come from animal-based products like meat, poultry, and fish.

Carbohydrates provide the energy needed to fuel a dog's activities. They can be found in grains, vegetables, and fruits. However, dogs do not have a requirement for carbohydrates and can get their energy from protein and fats alone.

Fats are an important source of energy and are necessary for the absorption of certain vitamins. They also play a crucial role in maintaining healthy skin and coat. Sources of fat in a dog's diet include meat, dairy, and plant-based oils.

Vitamins and minerals are necessary for many of the body's functions, such as bone growth, maintenance of the immune system, and regulation of the nervous system. Most quality dog foods include a variety of vitamins and minerals, but supplements may be needed if a dog has a particular health condition.

It is important to note that not all dogs have the same nutritional requirements. Large breed puppies, for example, require different levels of nutrients than senior dogs or dogs with specific health issues. It is important to consult with a veterinarian to determine the appropriate diet for a specific dog and to ensure they are getting all the necessary nutrients to maintain optimal health.

Feeding Your Dog

Feeding your dog is an important aspect of their overall health and wellbeing. When it comes to choosing the right food for your dog, it's important to consider their age, weight, and activity level. Many dog owners prefer to feed their dogs a commercial dog food, but it's important to choose a high-quality brand that contains all of the necessary nutrients.

If you're interested in feeding your dog a homemade diet, it's important to consult with a veterinarian or canine nutritionist to ensure that your dog is receiving all of the necessary nutrients. Homemade diets can be time-consuming and expensive and may not be appropriate for all dogs.

Regardless of whether you choose to feed your dog a commercial or homemade diet, it's essential to monitor their weight and adjust their food intake accordingly. Overfeeding can lead to obesity, which in turn can lead to a variety of health problems. On the other hand, underfeeding can lead to malnutrition and a wide range of health problems as well.

In addition to providing your dog with a balanced diet, it's essential to ensure that they always have access to clean, fresh water. Dogs tend to drink more water when they're eating a high-protein diet, so it's important to monitor their water intake and make sure that they're drinking enough.

Ultimately, feeding your dog is an important responsibility that should not be taken lightly. By providing your dog with a healthy, balanced diet, you can help to ensure that they live a long, healthy life.

Common Health Problems

As much as we love our furry friends, they are not immune to health problems. Some of the most common health issues faced by dogs include fleas and ticks, allergies, skin infections, ear infections, and dental problems.

Flea and tick infestations can lead to skin irritation and even disease. Preventative measures, such as topical or oral medications, can help keep your pet free of these pesky pests.

Allergies can affect dogs just like they can humans. Common dog allergies include allergies to fleas, environmental allergens such as pollen or dust, and ingredients in their food. Symptoms of allergies can include itching, redness, and even digestive problems.

Skin infections can occur due to allergies or other factors such as hot spots or wounds. They can be treated with medication prescribed by a veterinarian.

Ear infections are also common in dogs, particularly those with floppy ears. Symptoms include shaking of the head, scratching at the ears, and discharge. It?s important to have these infections diagnosed and treated by a vet as they can be quite painful for your pet.

Dental problems can lead to pain, infection, and tooth loss. Regular teeth cleaning and proper nutrition can help prevent these issues. If you notice any unusual symptoms in your dog such as lethargy, loss of appetite, or vomiting, it?s important to seek veterinary care right away. Early detection and treatment of health problems can help ensure a long and happy life for your furry friend.

Preventive Care

Preventive care is essential for ensuring your dog's long term health and well-being. This includes regular visits to the veterinarian for check-ups, vaccinations, and dental cleanings. Keeping your dog up-to-date on all necessary vaccinations can prevent the spread of diseases and help protect your dog from getting sick. Regular dental cleanings can also prevent dental disease, which can lead to serious health problems down the road.

In addition to regular veterinary care, maintaining a healthy diet and regular exercise helps prevent obesity and other health issues. Providing your dog with high-quality, nutrient-rich food and ensuring they receive the appropriate portions can help prevent weight gain and obesity. Regular exercise helps keep their muscles strong, supports healthy joints, and maintains overall cardiovascular health.

Environmental factors can also impact your dog's health. Regularly cleaning their living space, using non-toxic cleaning products, and keeping toxic substances out of your dog's reach can prevent accidental poisoning or exposure to harmful chemicals.

By taking a proactive approach to your dog's health, you can help prevent many common health issues and ensure that your furry friend lives a long, healthy life by your side.

Senior Care

As dogs age, their nutritional and health needs change. Senior dogs are more susceptible to health issues such as arthritis, obesity, and kidney disease, so it is important to adjust their diet accordingly. Senior dog food formulas are available and are specifically designed for dogs over the age of seven or eight years. These formulas contain lower levels of fat and calories while still providing all the necessary nutrients for senior dogs.

In addition to nutrition, exercise is also essential for senior dogs. Regular walks and light play can help maintain their muscle tone, joint mobility, and overall health. However, it is important to understand their limitations and adjust exercise routines according to their physical ability and health conditions.

Regular health check-ups are also crucial for senior dogs. They should be taken to the vet at least twice a year, and blood and urine tests should be performed to detect any underlying health issues. Dental health is also important, as dental problems can lead to other health issues. Senior dogs may also need to have their medication regimen adjusted as well.

Ultimately, providing the best possible senior care for dogs involves a combination of proper nutrition, exercise, regular check-ups, and attention to their specific health needs. With the right care, senior dogs can live a happy and healthy life.

Euthanasia

Euthanasia is a difficult decision that many pet owners may need to make at some point in their dog's life. It is important to understand what euthanasia means and how it is carried out.

Euthanasia is a painless way to end a dog's life and is a humane option when a dog is suffering from a terminal illness or debilitating condition that cannot be treated. Veterinarians are trained to carry out the procedure in a way that is as peaceful and painless as possible.

It is common for pet owners to struggle with the decision to euthanize their dog. It is important to remember that it is okay to seek support from loved ones and professionals during this difficult time. Some pet owners even choose to have a hospice care plan in place for their dog, which can help the dog to live out their remaining days comfortably and with as much quality of life as possible.

It is also important for pet owners to make sure they understand the laws and regulations around euthanasia in their area. Most areas require a veterinarian to carry out the procedure, and there may be specific requirements around timing and documentation.

Ultimately, the decision to euthanize a dog is a personal one that should be made in the best interests of the dog's well-being. While it can be an incredibly difficult choice, it can also be a compassionate option to relieve a dog's suffering and ensure they do not experience prolonged pain or discomfort.

Chapter 11

Developing the Art of Listening in Your Dog

Why Your Dog Refuses to Heed Your Orders

There are many reasons behind his or her decision to ignore you, but the top reasons are:

Not Acknowledging Your Dominance – If you're the alpha dog, your pet will follow whatever instruction you provide. However, if you relinquish that post by making any of the mistakes mentioned in the previous chapter, your dog will never listen to you. In fact, he'll expect you to abide by his commands and show signs of dominance and even aggression whenever necessary.

Not Knowing That You're Addressing Him – If your dog ignores you or doesn't show any reaction whenever you call his name, chances are that he doesn't know that you're talking to him. In this case, you'll need to train him to recognize his name and realize that you're addressing him.

Finding Someone or Something More Interesting – One of the reasons why your dog may not be listening to you is because they found someone or something else interesting. For example, while you're trying to train her, she may be distracted if a squirrel passes by or if your spouse, whom she apparently adores, heads in your direction.

Untimely Punishing Your Dog – If you use inappropriate forms of punishment or correct your dog at the wrong time, she won't understand the message you're sending and may even misinterpret it. For instance, if you punish your pet for returning home after running after a car, she'll think that your action is the result of coming back.

Requiring More Training – There's always a chance that your dog need to be re-trained because it doesn't remember basic teachings that help it connect to you. If you notice other mistakes, such as her not accepting a leash, you'll need a refresher training course.

If any of these have been preventing you from effectively connecting with your dog, you need to take action right away because old dogs don't learn new tricks. Besides, if she wouldn't listen to you, how can both of you communicate?

How to Be Heard

You're not the only one whose pet refuses to listen to them and heed their instructions. However, you need to take a firm step or else you'll lose the chance to have a well-behaved furry companion. The following are some of the best tips to be heard and ultimately get your message through.

Show Your Dog Who's in Charge – You need to show your dog that you're the alpha so that it can listen to you. This can be done through a number of actions like going out or coming in through the door first, eating first before feeding your dog, forcing your pet out of your way rather than circling them, and only paying attention when you think fit rather than when she demands it. These steps are necessary to help you train your dog and establish a bond where you get the upper hand.

Train Your Dog to Recognize His Name – If you get a blank look whenever you call your pooch, you need to train him to recognize his name. The easiest way to go for is by holding a doggy treat away from your body and calling your dog's name repeatedly until he looks into your eyes. Only award him the treat when he looks at you. With time, you can shift from offering treats to simply petting your dog or giving him a hug whenever he responds to you.

Choose the Right Timing – Timing is one of the essentials of teaching your dog how to listen. If he's too tired or if she's too full to be tempted by your treats, they'll not be interested in what you have to say. This may anger you and cause you to take rash action that will further affect your relationship rather than build it. So pick the right time to get your dog to actually listen to you.

Control Your Tone – Dogs have different sounds for different emotions and purposes, so you need to make sure that your tone reflects strength so that your dog can hear you. Compare saying (not shouting) "Fido, come" in a clear, happy and firm with "Oh my God,   in a soft, whiny sound. People will take you more seriously if you choose the first let alone an animal

Be Patient – It's quite easy to become angry or frustrated when your dog doesn't show response. However, as a leader, the last thing you should do is to lose your temper. Dogs tend to react according to what they see, so there's always a chance that she'll take matters in her own hands rather than let you guide her through.

Become More Interesting – You need to become the main focus of your dog's attention. This means that you should train him to listen in a distraction-free space and incorporate fun and new treats to help him understand that heeding your orders will give him the delicious or exciting reward you have in store.

Be Worth Listening To – Your dog will deem you worthy of her attention if you're confident, calm and decisive. Stick to any rule you make for your dog to ensure that she doesn't undermine your authority. This would also mean not giving in to "those eyes" she gives you.

Getting your dog to listen is never an easy task, especially if this is your first attempt at it. Therefore, always be patient and affirmative. Don't be repetitive; your dog won't respond the way you want him to if you keep stating the same thing again and again. Finally, enjoy the ride;

there will come a day when you'll reflect on the hours you had spent trying to understand one another.

Chapter 12

Getting to Know Your Dog

Individual Dog Personalities

Just like people, each dog has a distinct personality. This section explores common personality traits among dogs and helps you identify the unique characteristics that make your dog special. Recognizing your dog's personality is the first step towards tailoring your training approach to suit their individual needs.

Assessing Your Dog's Learning Style

Not all dogs learn in the same way. In this part of the chapter, we guide you through assessing your dog's learning style. Whether your dog is a visual, auditory, or kinesthetic learner, understanding their preferred learning method allows you to customise your training techniques for optimal results.

The Role of Breed and Background

Breed characteristics and your dog's background also play a significant role in their behaviour and learning tendencies. This section provides insights into how breed traits and previous experiences can influence your dog's responses to training. Discover how to leverage this knowledge to tailor your training sessions effectively.

Observing Behavioural Cues

Learning to interpret your dog's body language and behavioural cues is a crucial aspect of effective communication. We'll explore how to observe and understand the signals your dog is sending, helping you respond appropriately and strengthen the bond between you and your furry friend.

As you immerse yourself in Chapter 2, envision the journey of discovery that awaits you. By truly getting to know your dog, you set the stage for a training experience that is not only effective but also enriching for both you and your canine companion.

Chapter 13

Basic Techniques in Dog Treat Preparation

Baking Basics

Baking is a popular and satisfying method for making homemade dog treats. It allows you to make a range of textures and flavors while preserving the nutritional worth of the ingredients. Here's a guide to the baking skills you need to learn for making delicious and wholesome treats for your furry friend:

Preheating the Oven: Always warm your oven according to the recipe's directions. This ensures that the treats cook properly and achieve the desired thickness.

Choosing the Right Temperature: Different recipes may require different baking temperatures. Follow the directions given to achieve the best results. Most dog food recipes fall in the range of 325°F to 375°F (163°C to 190°C).

Using Dog-Safe Ingredients: Double-check that all items used in your recipes are safe for canine eating. Avoid ingredients like chocolate, onions, and excessive salt, which can be harmful to dogs.

Measuring Ingredients Accurately: Accurate numbers are important in baking. Use measuring cups and spoons to ensure that the amounts of ingredients are correct, keeping the treats' consistency.

Mixing Techniques: Mix ingredients fully, but avoid overmixing, which can lead to tough treats. For dry ingredients, use a whisk or fork, and for wet ingredients, use a spatula or spoon.

Rolling and Cutting Dough: If your method involves rolling out dough, use a lightly floured surface to avoid sticking. Use dog-friendly cookie cutters to cut shapes, making treats of uniform size.

Baking Time: Follow the recommended baking times in your recipes. Keep a close eye on treats toward the end of the baking time to avoid overcooking, which can result in a dry taste.

Cooling Treats: Allow treats to cool fully on a wire rack before serving or keeping. This stops condensation and ensures the treats keep their desired texture.

Storing Baked Treats: Store baked treats in sealed containers to maintain freshness. For longer shelf life, you can refrigerate or freeze treats, based on the recipe.

Experimenting with Flavors: Baking gives for a wide range of flavor choices. Experiment with different items like peanut butter, applesauce, and oats to find your dog's favorites.

No-Bake Options

No-bake dog treats are a handy and quick option to traditional baked treats. These recipes often involve minimal preparation and are great for hot days when you'd rather not turn on the oven.

Here's a guide to learning no-bake choices for your canine companion:

Selecting No-Bake Ingredients: Choose ingredients that work well without baking, such as oats, olive oil, peanut butter, and dried vegetables. These items provide taste and texture without the need for heat.

Mixing and Shaping: Combine items thoroughly using a mixing bowl and spoon. Once the mixture hits a dough-like consistency, shape it into bite-sized treats or use cookie cutters for more intricate patterns.

Cooling Time: No-bake treats often require cooling time to set. Place the shaped treats in the refrigerator for at least a couple of hours or until they firm up.

Portion Control: Keep in mind that no-bake treats can be more delicate than baked ones. Be aware of serving sizes to avoid overly sticky or gooey treats.

Adding Freeze-Dried Ingredients: Enhance the taste and nutrition of no-bake treats by adding freeze-dried ingredients like fruits or vegetables. These add a delicious crunch and intense taste.

Experimenting with Nut Butters: No-bake treats provide an excellent chance to try with different nut butters, such as almond or cashew butter. These add flavor and health benefits.

Storing No-Bake Treats: Store no-bake treats in the refrigerator to maintain their structure. Airtight packages or zip-top bags work well for keeping freshness.

Customizing for Allergies: No-bake recipes are easily adaptable for dogs with allergies. Substitute items as needed to suit your dog's dietary restrictions.

Freezing and Refrigeration Tips

Freezing and refrigerating dog treats can extend their shelf life and provide a cool choice for **your pup on hot days. Here are some tips for successful freezing and refrigeration:**

Choosing Freezable Ingredients: Select ingredients that freeze well, such as yogurt, pureed veggies, and soup. These ingredients can make icy treats that are great for cooling down your dog.

Popsicle Molds: Invest in dog-friendly popsicle molds for freezing treats. These molds come in different shapes and sizes, adding a fun element to frozen treats.

Layering tastes: Experiment with layering different tastes in popsicle shapes. For example, you can make a tiered treat with a yogurt base, followed by a fruit layer, and a final layer of broth.

Cooling Time: Pay attention to the suggested cooling times in your recipes. Overfreezing can make treats overly hard, while underfreezing may result in a messy and less enjoyable experience.

Single-Serving Portions: Freeze treats in single-serving portions to make it handy for serving and to avoid the need to thaw an entire batch at once.

Refrigerating Moist Treats: Treats with higher moisture content, such as those containing fresh fruits or veggies, are best kept in the refrigerator to avoid spoilage.

Thawing Frozen Treats: When offering frozen treats, allow them to thaw for a few minutes to make it easier for your dog to enjoy. Some dogs may prefer softer treats, while others enjoy the task of chewing on a partly frozen treat.

Using Ice Cube Trays: Ice cube trays are excellent for freezing small amounts of treats. This is particularly useful for making bite-sized frozen treats.

Avoiding Overfeeding: While frozen treats are a wonderful way to keep your dog cool, be aware of their caloric content. Adjust your dog's general diet to handle the extra calories from treats.

Safety Considerations: Always use safe items when making frozen treats. Avoid xylitol, sweets, and other chemicals that can be dangerous to dogs.

Mastering the basics of baking, exploring no-bake options, and utilizing freezing and cooling techniques open up a world of possibilities for creating homemade treats that cater to your dog's tastes and dietary needs. The future parts of this guide will dive into specific recipes, providing inspiration for lovely treats that will have your dog eagerly expecting every snack time.

Chapter 14

Instructing the "Tune in".

Comprehend the motivation behind the "tune in" order.

One of the first commands you should teach your dog is "listen," which is also known as the "watch me" command. You'll utilize it to stand out so you can provide him the following order or bearing. Certain individuals simply utilize their canine's name rather than the "tune in." If you have multiple dogs, this is especially helpful. Like that, every individual canine will know when you believe it should zero in on you.

Stand close to your canine.

However, do not interact with him. Stand still and look away if he reacts to your presence until he loses interest.

Speak slowly but firmly, "Listen."

Say your dog's name instead of using the "listen" or "watch me" commands when calling him by name. You should speak in the same manner and at the same volume as if you were calling someone's name to get their attention.

Give the desired response an immediate reward.

Give your dog praise and a treat as soon as he stops doing something and looks at you. Make the snap sound prior to giving commendation or a treat on the off chance that you're utilizing clicker preparing.

Keep in mind that you must respond right away. He will better comprehend the connection between command, behavior, and reward the faster you reward him.

At some point, stop buying candy.

Whenever he's dominated the order, you shouldn't give him treats for performing it; Nevertheless, you should still use your clicker or praise others verbally.

Weaning the canine off treats is significant on the grounds that he might begin to anticipate treats constantly. You'll wind up with a canine who possibly performs when you have food.

Even after your dog has mastered a command, you should praise and treat him on a regular basis. That will ensure that it remains ingrained in his dog vocabulary.

You can use treats to encourage faster or more accurate behavior once he has mastered command. He will before long understand that the treats accompany the order or movement that follows the "tune in."

Chapter 15

Unwanted behavior

Unwanted behavior in German Shepherds may be controlled with regular and constructive training approaches. Excessive barking is a prevalent problem.

To combat this, use instructions like "quiet" and treat silence. Similarly, leaping on people can be reduced by teaching and reinforcing the "off" command while all four paws are on the ground.

Another issue is aggression, which is typically motivated by fear or territorial tendencies.

Socialization is essential; start exposing your German Shepherd to different people, situations, and other dogs as soon as possible. To build favorable connections, reward calm conduct among strangers. Chewing and destructive habits can be reduced by providing adequate mental and physical stimulation.

To channel their energy productively, provide chew toys and participate in frequent exercise. When encountering undesired objects, reinforce the "leave it" instruction.

A steady schedule for feeding and restroom breaks might help with housebreaking issues. Outdoor elimination that is rewarded encourages the desired behavior. Indoor mishaps can be avoided with crate training.

In German Shepherd training, consistency is essential.

To quickly reward desirable behavior, use positive reinforcement strategies such as sweets and praise. German Shepherds thrive on cerebral stimulation; therefore, patience and recognizing their intellect are essential. If necessary, get expert training to ensure a healthy link between you and your faithful canine friend.

Your Dog's Reason for Bad Behavior

Understanding your dog's undesirable behavior is critical for effective training, especially if you have a breed like the German Shepherd, which is noted for its intellect and strong will. Lack of sociability, boredom, worry, or insufficient exercise are all common causes of undesirable conduct.

German Shepherds rely on mental and physical stimulation; therefore, a lack of involvement may result in destructive tendencies.

Create an organized training schedule that includes daily walks, play sessions, and cognitively challenging activities to address this.

Reinforce positive actions with goodies and praise to help your German Shepherd link good behavior with favorable consequences. Consistency is essential; inconsistent training might confuse your dog.

It is critical to socialize your German Shepherd by introducing him to a variety of situations, people, and other animals. This aids in the reduction of anxiety and fear-based behaviors.

Establish clear limits and standards in your house as well, creating a controlled setting that promotes good conduct.

Training methods should be compatible with your dog's disposition.

Positive reinforcement works well with German Shepherds, but strong leadership is required. Professional obedience lessons or employing a competent trainer can provide invaluable insights and hands-on training help.

Understanding the underlying reasons for your German Shepherd's negative behavior, along with constant training, enough exercise, and positive reinforcement, will result in a well-behaved and happy companion.

Refusing to come when Called Getting rid of Biting Behavior

Training a German Shepherd involves patience and perseverance, especially when dealing with issues such as refusal to come when called and biting.

To overcome command resistance, begin with basic obedience training in a supervised environment. When the dog reacts successfully, provide positive reinforcement, such as treats or praise, to strengthen the relationship between the command and a positive outcome.

To imitate real-world events, progressively add distractions during memory training. Punish for late answers while consistently rewarding timely responses. Make coming when called more appealing by incorporating alluring rewards. This builds trust and promotes the notion that obeying directions results in favorable experiences.

Understanding the breed's innate tendencies is essential for dealing with biting behavior.

Because German Shepherds are known for their protective instincts, channel their biting inclinations into appropriate chew toys.

If the dog bites while playing, stop the interaction immediately to teach boundaries. Consistency is essential, and encouraging positive behavior teaches the dog what is acceptable.

Additionally, to avoid boredom-related behaviors, participate in frequent physical and mental stimulation. To keep the German Shepherd active and less prone to display negative habits, provide a range of toys and activities. Positive reinforcement, persistence, and knowing the breed's tendencies will all help to produce a well-trained and well-behaved German Shepherd.

Biting and Mouthing Prevention

To prevent biting and mouthing in German Shepherds, consistent training and positive reinforcement are crucial. Start early, as puppies tend to explore the world with their mouths.

Provide appropriate chew toys to satisfy their natural urge to bite. When the puppy mouths on inappropriate objects or attempts to bite, redirect their attention to the approved toys. Reinforce good behavior by praising and rewarding it with treats.

Establish clear boundaries through commands like "no bite" or "gentle." If the puppy becomes too enthusiastic during play, cease interaction briefly to convey that biting results at the end of playtime.

Consistency is key to instilling these lessons effectively.Socialization is equally important. Expose your German Shepherd to various environments, people, and animals to reduce anxiety and fear-based aggression. Enroll in puppy training classes to enhance their obedience and social skills.

Teaching bite inhibition is a critical aspect of training. Gradually decrease the pressure of bites during play to help the dog understand the appropriate level of force.

Utilize positive reinforcement techniques, praising the dog for soft mouthing and issuing corrections for excessive pressure.

Incorporate daily exercise to channel their energy positively and reduce the likelihood of boredom-related biting.

Regular mental stimulation through interactive games and training sessions will contribute to a well-behaved German Shepherd.

Patience, consistency, and positive reinforcement form the foundation for successful biting and mouthing prevention in German Shepherd training.

Using Faith to Avoid Biting

Training a German Shepherd needs a variety of tactics, and religion may be an effective tool in reducing unwanted tendencies like biting.

Establish a consistent pattern for feeding, walking, and playing to create trust between you and your German Shepherd.

Predictability is important to dogs, particularly German Shepherds, and a scheduled routine may foster a sense of security, minimizing the chance of nervous or aggressive behavior.

When it comes to biting, confidence in the training process is essential. Use positive reinforcement tactics to promote excellent behavior by rewarding it with treats or praise.

To minimize misunderstandings, reinforce the same behaviors on a regular basis. If your German

Shepherd is biting, switch their focus to acceptable chew toys.

By doing so, you establish in children the belief that good behavior is not only rewarded but also delightful.

Patience is also required for faith. German Shepherds are bright, but they require time to teach.

Punishment-based tactics should be avoided since they might destroy trust and worsen behavioral disorders. Instead, be patient and continually reinforce favorable acts.

Including religion in German Shepherd training entails developing a pattern for consistency, using positive reinforcement to encourage good behavior, diverting biting tendencies, and remaining patient during the process. This all-encompassing approach fosters a strong link built on trust, which is vital for a well-behaved and content German Shepherd.

Getting Rid of Undesirable Behaviors

A diverse strategy is required to properly address unwanted habits while teaching a German Shepherd. Begin by creating regular directives and positive reinforcement to build clear communication.

To express expectations, use simple, firm indicators, encouraging desired actions with incentives or praise. Consistency is essential; repetition assists the dog in understanding and internalizing orders.

It is critical to redirect bad habits. Instead of penalizing undesirable conduct, shift the attention to a positive activity.

For example, if the dog frequently jumps on people, train them to sit and reward them for it. This not only discourages unwanted behavior, but it also encourages compliance and response. Socialization is really important. From a young age, expose the German Shepherd to a variety of surroundings, humans, and other animals.

This promotes flexibility and confidence, which aid in the prevention of aggressive or anxious behaviors.

This lively breed requires regular exercise. A weary dog is less likely to engage in unpleasant activities as a result of boredom or surplus energy. Include regular walks, playing, and mentally stimulating activities in their schedule.

Patience and positive reinforcement should be used to reinforce training. Avoid severe penalties, since positive reinforcement works better with German Shepherds. Build a bond based on trust and respect to build the human-dog bond.
Seek expert help if necessary. A professional dog trainer can give tailored solutions to your German Shepherd's unique issues, delivering a well-rounded and positive training experience.

Whining, Howling, and Excessive Barking are all Issues

Understanding German Shepherd behavior and applying appropriate training approaches are required to address whining, howling, and excessive barking. These vocalizations are frequently motivated by boredom, fear, or a need for attention.

To address these concerns, begin with regular exercise to constructively channel their energy. German Shepherds are bright and thrive on mental stimulation, so include tough toys and puzzles in their daily routine.

Create a consistent daily plan for feeding, exercise, and play to promote consistency and security. When dealing with whining or barking, refrain from responding quickly to prevent rewarding the habit. Instead, wait for a period of silence before rewarding them with praise or food. This teaches the dog that quiet conduct is more rewarding than loud activity.

During training sessions, use positive reinforcement approaches. Teach instructions such as "quiet" and "enough" and praise obedience.

Socialization is essential for reducing anxiety-driven vocalizations by introducing your German Shepherd to a variety of surroundings and people. When left alone, crate training can create a safe area for the dog and prevent excessive barking.

Maintain consistency by ensuring that all family members follow the same training rules. If concerns persist, seek professional help since they may signal underlying issues that require expert care.

Understanding your German Shepherd's requirements and using gentle, consistent training methods will help you effectively solve whining, howling, and excessive barking, resulting in a well-behaved and satisfied companion.

Chewing and Jumping on Others

Training a German Shepherd necessitates regular and positive reward strategies that cover a wide range of behaviors, including chewing and leaping.

To address chewing inclinations, appropriate chew toys are provided to refocus their natural impulse to nibble.

Praise and treat the dog when it chews on specific things to reinforce positive behavior. Consistency is essential to breaking bad chewing habits.

Begin with teaching the "sit" command to avoid leaping on others. Consistently reinforce this command, praising the dog when it obeys. Redirect the German Shepherd's attention to the "sit" command when it wants to leap, encouraging the desirable behavior. To urge the dog to stay calm and collected, use food and positive verbal signals.

Include leash training to help you keep control during interactions. Ask for their help in reinforcing the teaching by not promoting leaping when meeting new individuals.

Consistent corrections and positive reinforcement will teach the German Shepherd that calm conduct is praised and leaping is not.

Exercise on a regular basis to burn off surplus energy and reduce the chances of hyperactive behavior.

Enroll in obedience lessons to improve sociability skills and reinforce training in a safe setting. A well-trained German Shepherd may demonstrate acceptable chewing behavior and resist leaping on people by combining consistent directions, positive reward, and scheduled exercises. Remember that patience and perseverance are necessary components of good training.

The Straining Band is Tugging on the Leash

To assure a well-behaved and obedient companion, training a German Shepherd demands a rigorous approach. One typical issue that owners experience is leash training, in which the straining band tugs on the leash.

Begin by picking a proper leash and collar for the dog, making sure they are both comfortable. When the dog pulls, you must establish yourself as the leader by giving firm but gentle corrections.

Consistency is essential; encourage positive behavior with rewards and address bad conduct as soon as possible.

Begin training in a distraction-free setting, gradually introducing stimuli to help the dog concentrate. Use simple orders such as "sit" and "stay" to develop discipline. Stop and wait for the dog to release the strain as the leash tightens due to pulling. Refocus its attention on you and reward conformity.

Change up the exercise program to keep things interesting. Include short, delightful walks in your routine, gradually increasing the time as your dog grows more receptive.

To enhance the link between good behavior and incentives, use positive reinforcement like snacks or praise. Patience is essential; consistency and good reward will progressively reduce leash tugging behaviors.

Understanding the distinct traits of German Shepherds, such as their intelligence and drive to please, can help improve training results.

Owners may create a close relationship with their German Shepherd while imparting proper leash etiquette by establishing a clear communication channel and providing a pleasant training environment.

Getting Away From Roaming

Effective training is essential for preventing wandering behavior in German Shepherds. Begin by defining and regularly enforcing clear limits.

Use positive reinforcement tactics to praise your dog for remaining within boundaries. To reinforce the desired behavior, use food, praise, or toys.

Regular exercise is essential for German Shepherds because it relieves excess energy, which might lead to wandering inclinations.

A fatigued dog is less likely to go out on its own. In order to keep your German Shepherd

physically and intellectually pleased, incorporate daily walks, fun, and cerebral stimulation.
Commands such as "stay" and "come" are vital for regulating your dog's movements. Experiment with these commands in a variety of settings, gradually increasing distractions.

Positive reinforcement should be used to reward compliance in order to build their relationship with each other.

If your German Shepherd escapes, invest in suitable identification, such as a collar with ID tags and a microchip, to boost the chances of a safe return.

To keep better control during walks, consider employing a strong leash or harness.

Another important part of training is socialization. Introduce your German Shepherd to new people, creatures, and places to minimize fear and curiosity, which can contribute to wandering. Training requires consistency and patience; be persistent in reinforcing limits and instructions to guarantee a well-behaved and pleased German Shepherd.

www.ingramcontent.com/pod-product-compliance
Lightning Source LLC
LaVergne TN
LVHW010216070526
838199LV00062B/4617